1-5. "Several times," said Elizabeth worriedly, "I've heard that peculiar noise."

6. hedges
7. the weather
8. gardening
9. matchbox labels
10. wines

11. avidity
12. suitability
13. fragility
14. indolence
15. equality

16. aquiline
17. feline
18. canine
19. porcine
20. ferine

21. cursed
22. celery
23. Uncle George
24. repudiating
25. donate

26. Rome was not built in a day.
27. It's no use crying over spilt milk.
28. There are none so deaf as those who will not hear.
29. Man proposes but God disposes.
30. Dead men tell no tales.

31. supernatural
32. supercilious
33. supervise
34. supermarket
35. superintendent

36. viva voce
37. nil desperandum
38. kismet
39. crème de la crème
40. victor ludorum

41. civilly
42. terribly
43. prettily
44. uncannily
45. mightily

46. ridiculous
47. procedure
48. umbrella
49. lovable
50. sergeant

51. Ere
52. air
53. adze
54. heir
55. adds

56. danger
57. navy/army
58. jail
59. tortured
60. cut off

61. profit
62. predecessor
63. abundance
64. discontinue
65. dissent

66-70. Various answers are possible.

71. horrified
72. verify
73. transact
74. falsify
75. putrefy

76. This house is ours, not yours.
77. The poor cat's lost its tail.
78. Which of the cars is theirs?
79. One's got to look after one's possessions.
80. I'm sure that jacket's hers and not his.

81. question closely
82. a puzzle, filling in words from clues given
83. a promise that what is said is the truth
84. a weapon for shooting arrows
85. (usually) a race through fields and woods

86. Lincolnshire
87. Northamptonshire
88. Oxfordshire
89. Isle of Wight
90. Shropshire

91. havoc/chaos
92. flag
93. violin (or cello)
94. the stars
95. nickname

96. geese
97. gooses
98. gooseries
99. gooseberries
100. goosefoots

1. "Is my tea ready?" Sam asked his mother.
2. "Mother," asked Sam, "is my tea ready?"
3. Sam asked his mother if his tea was ready.
4. "Is my tea ready, mother?" asked Sam.
5. "I'm starving to death!" Sam cried dolefully.

6. <u>lenient</u>
7. <u>raze</u>
8. <u>flower</u>
9. <u>gallon</u>
10. <u>merchant</u>

11. wine
12. window in a roof
13. horn
14. explosives
15. Easter

16. geniality
17. euphoria
18. convention
19. abhorrence
20. fervour

21. We gave our loaves to the enemies' allies.
22. Their ravenous oxen devoured our potato crops.
23. They used their scissors to cut the sheep's wool.
24. The passers-by took the sharp knives from the children.
25. The dingoes chased the kangaroos across the plateaux/plateaus.

26. overdone
27. rent
28. rewound
29. rewritten
30. slid

31. dext(e)rous
32. addictive
33. disdainful
34. lucrative
35. oriental

36. automobile
37. violoncello
38. gymnasium
39. spectacles
40. promenade

41. The Devil makes work for idle hands.
42. You cannot have your cake and eat it.
43. Everything comes to him who waits.
44. A fair exchange is no robbery.
45. What the eye does not see the heart does not grieve over.

46. queueing
47. parallel
48. picnicked
49. irresistible
50. corroborate

51. yellow
52. orange
53. purple
54. green
55. brown

56. Canberra, Dollar
57. Helsinki, Markka
58. Copenhagen, Krone
59. Brasilia, Cruzeiro
60. Quito, Sucre

61. grille
62. lowed
63. Load
64. grill
65. lode

66. Echo
67. Morpheus
68. Judas
69. Achilles'
70. Shakespeare

71. lakes
72. rabbits
73. newspapers
74. doctors
75. condiments

76. Messieurs
77. Justice of the Peace
78. Her (His) Majesty's Government
79. Member (of the Order) of the British Empire
80. general practitioner

81. people paid to work on behalf of the country
82. a war between people of the same country
83. the rights of a citizen to personal freedom
84. the sum of money voted by Parliament for the royal family
85. law concerning quarrels between people

86. Pisa
87. Wednesday
88. Ben Nevis
89. Pilgrim Fathers
90. Wales

91. flautist
92. violinist
93. cellist
94. timpanist
95. pianist

96. <u>crook</u> and <u>nanny</u> → nook and cranny
97. <u>Sheets</u> and <u>Kelley</u> → Keats and Shelley
98. <u>tasted</u> the whole <u>worm</u> → wasted the whole term
99. <u>shoving leopard</u> → loving shepherd
100. half-<u>warmed fish</u> → half-formed wish

1-5. "Dad's hammer's missing," moaned Sam, "so I can't fix those new planks on the shed for Mrs Goodwin's mother."

6. browse
7. down-and-out
8. regret
9. criticise
10. wax

11. minimum
12. synonym
13. Antarctic
14. rudeness
15. primitive

16. freeze
17. jamb
18. frees
19. jam
20. frieze

21. those
22. these
23. us
24. our
25. their

26. Everest
27. thirty-one
28. Maoris
29. vaccination
30. one hundred and five

31. a flask for carrying gunpowder
32. a boy carrying powder to the gunners on a ship of war
33. a soft ball for dusting powder on the skin
34. a ladies cloakroom/a ship's powder magazine
35. be ready for action

36. carelessness
37. dilemma
38. arsonist
39. ruddy
40. senseless

41. festivity
42. contravention
43. abstinence/abstention
44. convalescence
45. dramatist

46. crockery
47. aquarium
48. acrobat
49. quill
50. kaleidoscope

51. either hand/both hands
52. communal farming settlement
53. projects into the sea
54. Scottish/Irish, English
55. different length

56. enigmatic
57. neurotic
58. emphatic
59. rhythmic
60. dogmatic

61. hypodermic
62. hypocaust
63. hypochondriac
64. hypotenuse
65. hypothermia

66. twenty-two
67. one hundred and thirty-two
68. twenty-six
69. two
70. one thousand, one hundred and eight

71. covey
72. flight
73. flock
74. host
75. posse

76. better
77. best
78. smaller
79. smallest
80. greediest

81. reflect
82. pan
83. supply
84. van
85. list

86. pastime
87. secretary
88. theatre
89. wholly
90. argument

91. oboist
92. organist
93. clarinettist
94. trombonist
95. accompanist/accompanyist

96. Having lost the key to her door, Mary was unable to get in.
97. Having done her shopping, Mrs Jones caught the bus home.
98. Having mown (mowed) the lawn, Siama then planted some bulbs.
99. Having read the question, George began to write.
100. Having decided that the derelict building was unsafe, the surveyors ordered it to be demolished.

	NOUN	ADVERB	VERB	ADJECTIVE
1.	sufficiency	sufficiently	SUFFICE	sufficient
2.	COMPREHENSION	comprehensively	comprehend	comprehensive
3.	resolution	resolutely	RESOLVE	resolute
4.	idleness	idly	IDLE	idle
5.	sympathy	sympathetically	sympathise	SYMPATHETIC

6.   fireman
7.   lector
8.   finale
9.   Hades
10. deep

11. only a remote chance of success
12. a fielder at cricket
13. favourable in terms of potential gain, unfavourable in terms of risk
14. tediously wordy
15. prolonged/unduly protracted

16. covert
17. Neptune
18. Napoleon
19. officer
20. war

21. buggy
22. shred
23. arbitrator
24. mum
25. utter

26. Cheshire cat
27. witness
28. schoolmaster
29. treasury
30. gadget

31. good
32. good/bad
33. bad
34. good
35. bad

36. furniture
37. gases
38. abodes
39. spirits
40. dogs

41. sub rosa
42. inter alia
43. in loco parentis
44. cave
45. curriculum vitae

46. neutral → mutual
47. exposition → expedition
48. intimate → intricate
49. vocation → vacation
50. pharmacist → pessimist

51-55. ''Dr Clark's nephew will be here at two o'clock tomorrow,'' promised Henry's mother, ''and I'll be glad to see him.''

56. port
57. many
58. exhale
59. return
60. aft

61. A tabloid is a popular newspaper, smaller sized, with many pictures.
62. A centaur was a mythical monster, half man, half horse.
63. A fjord is a narrow inlet of the sea between steep cliffs.
64. Another word for medley is selection/miscellany.
65. A cutlass was a short, broad sword often used by seamen.

66. grizzlies
67. larvae
68. funguses or fungi
69. lavatories
70. gypsies (or gipsies)

71. bear
72. fox
73. lion
74. badger
75. cat

76. slam
77. hiss
78. crack
79. jingle
80. skirl

81. haemophilia
82. pseudonym
83. archaeology
84. automobile
85. ultrasound

86. surge
87. vain
88. vein
89. serge
90. vane

91. blue
92. yellow
93. yellow
94. green
95. red

96. manageable
97. committed
98. forty-two
99. association
100. humorous

1. clothing
2. brave
3. competent
4. euphoric
5. jovial

6. suddenness
7. emergence
8. magnificence
9. antiquity
10. peculiarities

11. The yolk of an egg is yellow.
12. The whole library of books was destroyed by fire.
13. Which of the two reds is nearer the pocket?
14. Who's coming with Jim and me to the party?
15. The soldiers attacked the guerrilla camp to free their colonel who had been held as a hostage for more than a week.

16. bowler
17. reader
18. loser
19. recipient
20. diner

21. medicine
22. islands
23. halo
24. nose
25. signal

26. graffiti
27. libretti or librettos
28. itineraries
29. discrepancies
30. ours or mines

31. impudence
32. polecat
33. Alsatian
34. artisan
35. unnerve

36. fossils
37. birds
38. fish
39. water (resources)
40. skin

41. purple
42. red
43. yellow
44. brown
45. black

46. a self-important official
47. will-o'-the-wisp/a lantern made from a pumpkin
48. a money pool in a competition
49. a breed of small terrier
50. a person who climbs tall chimneys, steeples etc. to do repairs

51. Yasmin asked Mary if she might borrow her pen.
52. In a gruff voice the security guard asked what I was doing.
53. The gamekeeper shouted at the poacher to halt or he would set the dogs on him.
54. Becky's mother asked if she thought she was made of money.
55. A neighbour asked me to come in and make myself at home.

56. cowl
57. limp
58. wash
59. must
60. harry

61. dog
62. fox
63. wolf (or pig)
64. badger
65. ram

66. chivalrous
67. Organic
68. pretentious
69. vituperative
70. graphic

71. agreeable
72. courageous
73. excessive
74. vicious
75. thorough

76. weigh
77. whey
78. way
79. wear
80. ware, warehouse

81. arrive, welcome, depart
82. hope, hop
83. take
84. raise, raze, rues, rise
85. box, shape, signal, brush, comb, holiday

86. pilot
87. pillion
88. copra
89. nougat
90. smith

91. court
92. feather
93. wheel
94. ski
95. plain

96. felon
97. meat
98. ire
99. departure
100. donate

1. lean
2. mole
3. poke
4. stoop
5. quick

6-10. ''His excellency the Count of Boravia, madam,'' announced Jenkins the butler in a sepulchral voice.

11. contradict
12. contraflow
13. contretemps
14. contravene
15. contraband

16. repulsive
17. mutinous
18. reptilian
19. symmetrical
20. asymmetrical

21. Arthur's father's friend
22. the fleet's manoeuvres
23. Mary Poppins' umbrella
24. Jones's
25. the gateau's taste

26. slung
27. slunk
28. smitten
29. spat
30. unbound

31. musician/actor/entertainer
32. count
33. wall
34. bicycle for two
35. hole in a barrel/container

36. disc
37. black
38. rain
39. grand
40. man

41. precede
42. persecute
43. populous
44. proceed
45. populace

46. twentieth
47. eleventh
48. first
49. sixteenth
50. ninth

51. Numbers
52. Gobi
53. Armley
54. Etna
55. Branwell

56. serious
57. carpenter
58. craven
59. indicate
60. mandarin

61. alopecia
62. cuboid
63. venomous
64. professional
65. reveal

66. migration
67. expression
68. perusal
69. intention
70. recession

71. the eyes
72. animal life
73. heart functions/diseases
74. mankind
75. the mind

76. blue
77. red
78. white
79. brown
80. purple

81. Middlesex
82. Derbyshire
83. Wiltshire
84. Buckinghamshire
85. West Yorkshire

86. (in cricket) a ball which does not bounce before reaching the batsman
87. a wrestling hold
88. having a high opinion of oneself
89. completely qualified
90. the moon when it is all visible

91. convex
92. optimism
93. zenith
94. emigrant
95. longitude

96. synchronise
97. unison
98. equinox
99. hemisphere
100. manuscript

1. milk
2. sand
3. witch
4. day
5. hard

6-10. Various answers are possible.

11. fourteenth
12. seventeenth
13. seventeenth
14. twentieth
15. seventeenth

16. astonished
17. disturb
18. damage
19. flinch
20. not distinctive

21. God and religion
22. rocks
23. (the origin of) words
24. growing old
25. diseases

26. ultra heat treated
27. Brothers
28. Roman Catholic
29. Queen's Police Medal
30. unidentified flying object

31. biannual
32. bicycle
33. bilingual
34. bifocal
35. bigamy

36. respect
37. criminal
38. nose
39. fence
40. letter

41. Arabic
42. English
43. English
44. Dutch
45. Danish

46. I bore Robert no ill-will for the problem that arose.
47. I was awakened each morning by the dawn chorus which began early.
48. She blew her whistle as the game drew to a close.
49. Tasmin ate and drank and then lay down.
50. The vandals ran and tore down anything they chose.

51. Both players scored forty points.
52. The second time the black dog appeared, I ran.
53. Several interesting features appeared in the new magazine.
54. "I don't believe either story," said Richard. "They're both stupid."
55. Many may apply for the exciting job but few will be chosen.

56. As Phillip was crossing the road, he saw Anne enter the shop.
57. As Mrs Briggs was reading, she heard the telephone ring.
58. As William climbed over the stile, the bull saw him.
59. As the burglar crept into the house, he tripped over the cat.
60. As Felix the cat slept soundly, the burglar tripped over him.

61. addressee
62. employee
63. trainee
64. devotee
65. refugee

66. heir
67. humane
68. hare
69. hair
70. human

71. pursuer
72. repetition
73. cemetery
74. buoy
75. insistent

76. Mary (1)   Mavis (3)   Maureen (2)   Millicent (4)   Miranda (5)
77. Murdoch (5)   Morgan (4)   Mark (1)   Matthew (2)   Melvin (3)
78. O'Dwyer (3)   Oliver (4)   O'Brien (1)   O'Reilly (5)   Odell (2)
79. Macbride (1)   McEnroe (5)   Macdonald (2)   Macpherson (3)   McCormack (4)
80. threshold (3)   three (2)   threat (1)   through (5)   throng (4)

81. John Keats
82. W H Auden
83. Lewis Carroll
84. Alfred Noyes
85. Walter de la Mare

86. eligible
87. fourth
88. diaphragm
89. notorious
90. proscribed

91. to be dealt with severely
92. exactly equal
93. a narrow or obstructed place in a road where traffic builds up
94. to work extremely hard
95. to put yourself at risk

96. immortal
97. intolerable
98. extrovert
99. irreverent
100. unnecessary

1.	high	56.	blue
2.	nose	57.	purple
3.	dog	58.	yellow
4.	heart	59.	black
5.	knock	60.	green

6. biography
7. biographer
8. biology
9. biologist
10. biopsy

61. a weapon (discharged by explosion)/a gun
62. stop fighting
63. hotly protesting
64. family insignia/heraldic bearings of a gentleman
65. protective covering, usually metal

11. the common people
12. coronation
13. sundial, shadow
14. pleasure
15. vertical

66. homeless
67. hopeless
68. fearless
69. Selfless
70. senseless

16. Peruvian
17. British
18. Portuguese
19. Norwegian
20. Finnish

71. wasps
72. ants
73. bees
74. birds
75. squirrels

21. liaise
22. distil
23. vilify
24. fortify
25. rectify

76. plasticine
77. harmless
78. boorish
79. melodrama
80. sir

26. very high frequency
27. as soon as possible
28. cash with order
29. Director of Public Prosecutions
30. (Officer of the) Order of the British Empire

81. lying
82. lain
83. laid
84. laid
85. laid

31. barrack
32. fast
33. cower
34. gamble
35. observation

86. ''My name is Clare,'' said the new girl in the class.
87. ''Can you tell me the way to the park?'' asked the tourist.
88. ''Would you like a cup of tea?'' Sheila asked the tramp.
89. ''Your work is disgraceful,'' the teacher told John.
90. ''May I have some more pudding, Mother?'' asked Sarah.

36-40. ''Charles Dickens wrote many books,'' Mrs Evans said, ''but my personal favourite is 'A Tale of Two Cities'.''

91. retreat/recede
92. loosen
93. factual
94. smoothness/gentleness
95. sanity

41. repugnance
42. irreligious
43. anemone
44. adamant
45. equator

96. The milk was collected and taken to the dairy.
97. A wooden partition separated the two areas.
98. The blow to his temple caused him to suffer from concussion.
99. The prodigal son wasted his money and then asked for paternal forgiveness.
100. ''You're such an idiot,'' Mrs Moore said crossly to her spouse.

46. impunity
47. immunity
48. illusion
49. allusion
50. delusion

51. The quick brown fox jumped over the lazy goose.
52. Whenever Midas touched an object, it turned to gold.
53. Icarus flew too high in the sky and the wax on his wings melted.
54. He fell to his death in the sea below.
55. I'm not letting any Tom, Dick or Harry play with my football.

1. war
2. window
3. full
4. fire
5. table

6. twentieth
7. seventeenth
8. sixth
9. fifteenth
10. eighteenth

11. changeable
12. knowledgeable
13. noticeable
14. marriageable
15. manageable

16. transit
17. transient
18. translucent/transparent
19. transact
20. transport

21. nut-brown
22. pitch-black
23. slate-grey
24. blood-red
25. bottle-green

26. a building at the gateway to an estate
27. one who watches over the opening and shutting of a gate
28. one who enters without being invited
29. a post from which a gate is hung
30. the price paid for admission

31. one's better half
32. to do the dirty on
33. just what the doctor ordered
34. at loggerheads
35. at a loose end

36. British Boxing Board of Control
37. video cassette recorder
38. British United Provident Association
39. compact disc/Corps Diplomatique/Civil Defence
40. date of birth

41. the governesses' philosophies
42. the jumbos' capacities
43. the physicians' diagnoses
44. the medicine-men's prognoses
45. the druggists' dispensaries

46. cuspidor
47. delta
48. kookaburra
49. Isaac
50. lucid

51. butterflies and moths
52. bad breath
53. lying
54. summary
55. wheel on its axle

56. immobility
57. mandatory
58. minority
59. potential
60. delicacy

61. Clint drove the cattle to the river and they swam across.
62. The joiner came and did what was needed to be done.
63. She shook her head as she rode the dilapidated bicycle.
64. I wrote to my friend when I got home.
65. He knew as he sang and rang the bell that people hated the noise he made.

66. lessen
67. shutter
68. curator
69. flummox
70. quotidian

71. nefarious
72. tureen
73. trimaran
74. vapid
75. incessant

76. paper
77. teeth
78. counties
79. scales
80. schools

81. When Ruth saw her husband, she ran forward to greet him.
82. When I heard the crash, I rushed to see what had happened.
83. When the milkman knocked at the door, he asked for his money.
84. When Martha saw the cottage, she liked it very much.
85. When the train arrived, Ahmar saw that it was empty.

86. crows
87. eagles
88. starlings
89. owls
90. swans

91. pictures/symbols
92. a powerful and wealthy business person
93. a bishop
94. as rich as Croesus
95. good/genuine/sure

96. ''Excuse me,'' whispered the old lady. ''May I please pass?''
97. ''I can't get through,'' the old lady muttered.
98. The old lady said that she could not get past.
99. ''I can't,'' barked the old lady, ''get past!''
100. ''Shift!'' roared the old lady.

1.   amphibious
2.   widower
3.   derelict
4.   epidemic
5.   neutral/impartial

6.   Heath Robinson
7.   Stygian
8.   Draconian
9.   Brobdingnagian
10. labyrinthine

11. a diver who fishes for pearl-oysters
12. a costermonger whose costume is decorated with pearl buttons
13. the entrance to Heaven
14. a US naval base attacked by the Japanese on 7th December 1941
15. to offer valuable or beautiful things to those who don't appreciate them

16. the dormice's difficulties
17. the apothecaries' pharmacies
18. the armies' phalanxes/phalanges
19. marvellous phenomena
20. ephemera

21. barber
22. tanner
23. haberdasher
24. fletcher
25. pawnbroker

26. perfect or ideal
27. winged horse in Greek legend
28. grappling-iron/hooking or grasping device
29. rage
30. puzzle or riddle

31. dehydration
32. scuttle
33. personage
34. epaulette
35. euphemism

36. Cypriot
37. Parisian/Parisienne
38. Mancunian
39. Liverpudlian
40. Glaswegian

41. pink
42. tattoo
43. compound
44. mufti
45. retort

46. overloaded/sunk
47. Ten Commandments
48. policeman
49. punishment/criticism
50. stealing

51-55. ''That was an interesting excuse,'' said Mrs Walters with a smile, ''but I'm afraid I don't believe a word of it.'' Henry scowled but said nothing.

56. forehead is a forelock
57. forecast
58. forebode
59. foregone
60. Forewarned is forearmed.

61. curling
62. momentous
63. Wordsworth
64. cycle
65. Anaemia

66. printing
67. history
68. angling/fishing
69. poetry
70. medicine

71. Edward Lear
72. William Blake
73. John Masefield
74. T S Eliot
75. Walter de la Mare

76-80. Various answers are possible.

81. Although it was after nine o'clock, Paul still dawdled to school.
82. Although Mr Briggs was ninety years old, he walked to town and back every day.
83. Although Alice had the flu, she insisted on going to work.
84. Although Jane and Jill were sisters, they did not get on well.
85. Although the rest of the menu looked appetising, Ian still preferred chicken.

86. garret/loft or an attic
87. studio
88. vestry
89. refectory
90. theatre

91. post
92. check
93. child
94. draw
95. ice

96. mum
97. rotor
98. reviver
99. level
100. deified

1. Herculean
2. lilliputian
3. saturnine
4. Rhadamanthine
5. philistine

6. speed
7. wagons
8. indigestion
9. shell of a crab, tortoise etc.
10. carefully/closely

11. requiring a lot of time to be spent
12. objects of the present put in the foundations of a building to be found later
13. an imaginary machine to travel through time
14. to make speedy progress on a journey
15. a time within which something has to be done

16. Reveille
17. ruminant
18. sceptre
19. scarlatina
20. yahoo

21. boudoir
22. atrium
23. annexe/annex
24. larder/pantry
25. dormitory

26. Indian
27. house
28. key
29. pea
30. quick

31. raiders
32. abhorrent
33. navigator
34. wonderment
35. Ulster

36. undergone
37. undertaken
38. waylaid
39. withstood
40. wrung

41. hurries
42. worries
43. tarries
44. carries
45. ferries

46. malodorous → melodious
47. Mouldy → Molten; flowered → flowed; corrupting → erupting
48. lavatory → laboratory; tubercular → tubular
49. electrocution → elocution
50. incinerator → incubator

51. intercede
52. interval, interlude
53. intercept
54. international
55. interfere

56. capacious/commodious
57. taxidermy
58. atheist
59. pore
60. infallible

61. outline
62. adorn
63. layer
64. authorisation
65. dawdler

66. constituency
67. a drone
68. a brazier
69. wine
70. a sombrero

71. omnipotent
72. omniscient
73. omnivorous, omnivore
74. omnibus
75. omnipresent

76. Albert
77. Prime Minister
78. rear
79. wealthy
80. churn

81. raised
82. rose
83. risen
84. raised
85. rose

86. vase
87. punnet
88. decanter
89. cruet
90. scuttle

91. composure
92. legality
93. Forethought
94. decorum
95. tenacity

96. to laugh up one's sleeve
97. to tilt at windmills
98. to burn one's boats
99. to go at it hammer and tongs
100. to wear one's heart on one's sleeve

1.	dynamo		51.	welcome
2.	octopus		52.	tend
3.	barometer		53.	soporific
4.	miller		54.	dusk
5.	pulpit		55.	deny

6.	hypocritical → Hippocratic		56.	squeak
7.	diseased → deceased		57.	Remus
8.	Phoenician → venetian		58.	Joan
9.	distinguisher → extinguisher		59.	Juliet
10.	Conservatory → Conservative		60.	Horsa

11.	misanthropist		61.	ingenuity
12.	miscarriage		62.	drudgery
13.	mischievous		63.	mimicry
14.	mistake		64.	antagonism
15.	mispronounce		65.	preference

16.	neither one thing nor another		66.	W H Davies
17.	someone in an unsuitable situation		67.	G K Chesterton
18.	one who sells fish		68.	Rudyard Kipling
19.	an awkward mess		69.	Lewis Carroll
20.	a flat piece of metal joining railway lines		70.	Lord Tennyson

21.	outmoded		71.	silent
22.	easy		72.	Mary Rose
23.	festival		73.	Dracula
24.	vineyard		74.	kleptomaniac
25.	bolt		75.	Florence Nightingale

26.	hay		76.	pilots
27.	fire		77.	golf clubs
28.	eggs		78.	US states
29.	corn		79.	artists
30.	actors		80.	antelopes

31.	quiver		81.	latterly
32.	creel		82.	envelop
33.	kitbag		83.	formally
34.	scabbard		84.	formerly
35.	sheath		85.	envelope

36-40.	"We'd better go," Chris muttered, "or he'll dock an hour's wages."		86.	listener
			87.	client
			88.	reader
41.	fleeing		89.	quarry
42.	flowed		90.	subject
43.	flew			
44.	fled		91.	custodial
45.	flown		92.	fortieth
			93.	(in)flammable
46.	to roll out the red carpet		94.	learned
47.	to tip somebody the wink		95.	satisfactory
48.	to be on tenterhooks			
49.	to be sitting pretty		96-	
50.	by hook or by crook		100.	Various answers are possible.